THE
PANIC
ROOM

PANIC, ANXIETY, AND THE
ART OF LYING TO EVERYONE

STUDY GUIDE

TROY MAXWELL

Scripture quotations marked KJV are taken from the King James Version of the Bible. Public domain. Scripture quotations marked NIV are taken from the Holy Bible, New International Version®, NIV®. Copyright © 1973, 1978, 1984, 2011 by Biblica, Inc.™ Used by permission of Zondervan. All rights reserved worldwide. www.zondervan.com. The "NIV" and "New International Version" are trademarks registered in the United States Patent and Trademark Office by Biblica, Inc.™ | Scripture quotations marked NKJV are taken from the New King James Version®. Copyright © 1982 by Thomas Nelson. Used by permission. All rights reserved. | Scripture quotations marked TLB are taken from The Living Bible copyright © 1971 by Tyndale House Foundation. Used by permission of Tyndale House Publishers Inc., Carol Stream, Illinois 60188. All rights reserved. The Living Bible, TLB, and The Living Bible logo are registered trademarks of Tyndale House Publishers. | Scripture quotations marked NLT are taken from the Holy Bible, New Living Translation, copyright © 1996, 2004, 2015 by Tyndale House Foundation. Used by permission of Tyndale House Publishers, Inc., Carol Stream, Illinois 60188. All rights reserved. | Scripture quotations marked MSG are taken from THE MESSAGE, copyright © 1993, 1994, 1995, 1996, 2000, 2001, 2002 by Eugene H. Peterson. Used by permission of NavPress. All rights reserved. Represented by Tyndale House Publishers, Inc. | Scripture quotations marked GNT are from the Good News Translation in Today's English Version—Second Edition. Copyright © 1992 by American Bible Society. Used by Permission.

For foreign and subsidiary rights, contact the author.

Interior Photos: © Shutterstock, Andrew van Tilborgh, Jessica Hegland, Dominic Fondon

ISBN: 978-1-950718-55-9   1 2 3 4 5 6 7 8 9 10

Printed in the United States of America

THE PANIC ROOM

PANIC, ANXIETY, AND THE
ART OF LYING TO EVERYONE

STUDY GUIDE

TROY MAXWELL

CONTENTS

THE COLLISION

"My life was about to collide with a reality that challenged everything about my self-perception, my marriage, and my abilities as a leader."

READING TIME

Read Chapter 1: "The Collision," in *The Panic Room.* Use the notes space to record any thoughts you want to remember or questions you want to talk about later.

Have you ever had a collision with a realization or circumstance that brought your leadership to a halt? What did you learn from this experience?

_____

_____

_____

_____

_____

_____

How have your loved ones helped in alerting you to your own physical limitations, your need to slow down, or other warning signs in your life?

_____

_____

_____

_____

_____

_____

Why do you think it's so difficult for many leaders to admit their own limitations and weaknesses? What do we believe is at stake if we can't do all or be all we desire to be?

_____

_____

_____

_____

_____

_____

_____

STUDY SCRIPTURE

Read Psalm 6:1-4

"LORD, do not rebuke me in your anger, or discipline me in your wrath.

Have mercy on me, LORD, for I am faint; heal me, LORD, for my bones are in agony.

My soul is in deep anguish.

How long, LORD, how long?

Turn, LORD, and deliver me; save me because of your unfailing love."

Have you ever come to a place in which you had no choice but to be honest with yourself (or God) about the fact that you were suffering? What brought you to that place?

_____

_____

_____

_____

Do you see elements of church culture, or Christian culture in general, that discourage authenticity—especially for ministry leaders? What are they?

_____

_____

_____

_____

Did you identify with any of Pastor Troy's thoughts or emotions in this chapter? Explain your answer.

_____

_____

_____

_____

Why do you think believers sometimes attribute weakness or suffering to spiritual forces without truly examining the physical factors involved?

_____

_____

_____

_____

_____

Think back to a time in which you were sick, incapacitated, or otherwise unable to fulfill your normal leadership responsibilities. Who stepped in and took the reins for you? Who gave you time and space to get better?

_____

_____

_____

_____

Now, think about who you step in for—who can rely on you when they're unable to take another step? Who are you supporting in the same way?

_____

_____

_____

_____

SHARE YOUR STORY

"A heavy sense of confusion and failure came with me. Here I am, the spiritual leader of the church and I couldn't do what I'm supposed to, I thought."

What's one practical step you can take this week to establish or strengthen your relationships with these support people? How can you ensure that, the next time you are unwell, you have a plan in place to ask for help and rely on others?

_____

_____

_____

_____

_____

_____

What other takeaways or initial thoughts do you have after reading about Pastor Troy's experience?

_____

_____

_____

_____

_____

_____

CHAPTER 2

SURVIVING CHILDHOOD

"I didn't know a thing about God, but that became my prodigal son moment. Somehow, some way, I would do everything I could to avoid the path my father was on."

READING TIME

Read Chapter 2: "Surviving Childhood," in *The Panic Room.* Use the notes space to record any thoughts you want to remember or questions you want to talk about later.

How do you think your upbringing has positively affected the way in which you lead?

_____

_____

_____

_____

_____

_____

_____

How do you think your upbringing has negatively affected the way in which you lead?

_____

_____

_____

_____

_____

_____

_____

How do you think Pastor Troy's upbringing affected the way that he led and the pressures he put on himself as an adult?

_____

_____

_____

_____

_____

_____

_____

STUDY SCRIPTURE

Read Galatians 5:16-26

"So I say, walk by the Spirit, and you will not gratify the desires of the flesh. For the flesh desires what is contrary to the Spirit, and the Spirit what is contrary to the flesh. They are in conflict with each other, so that you are not to do whatever you want. But if you are led by the Spirit, you are not under the law.

The acts of the flesh are obvious: sexual immorality, impurity and debauchery; idolatry and witchcraft; hatred, discord, jealousy, fits of rage, selfish ambition, dissensions, factions and envy; drunkenness, orgies, and the like. I warn you, as I did before, that those who live like this will not inherit the kingdom of God.

But the fruit of the Spirit is love, joy, peace, forbearance, kindness, goodness, faithfulness, gentleness and self-control. Against such things there is no law. Those who belong to Christ Jesus have crucified the flesh with its passions and desires. Since we live by the Spirit, let us keep in step with the Spirit. Let us not become conceited, provoking and envying each other."

Think back on your childhood experiences. Is there anything you began to run away from, just as Pastor Troy made it his mission to never live the immoral life of his father?

_____

_____

_____

_____

What contrasts do you see in the character of Pastor Troy's father? Are there any positive attributes that stand out to you?

_____

_____

_____

_____

_____

How do you think it affected Pastor Troy to have little to no predictability in his relationship with his parents? How do you think that influenced his mindset as an adult?

_____

_____

_____

_____

Have you ever had a "wake up" moment like Pastor Troy did in front of the mirror—a moment when you decided to change directions, let something go, or pursue a new path? What led you to that realization?

_____

_____

_____

_____

What role do you see Pastor Troy's friends and other acquaintances playing in his journey as a young man?

_____

_____

_____

_____

_____

_____

_____

_____

How can you take steps toward improving the quality of your relationships, and surrounding yourself with people you want to be like?

_____

_____

_____

_____

_____

_____

_____

Does anything else stand out to you from Pastor Troy's account in this chapter?

_____

_____

_____

_____

_____

DIAGNOSING THE VOODOO

"My mind ran through so many possibilities. Did I have sin I needed to confess? Was this divine punishment? If not, why would God let me experience this? Wasn't I giving my life to serve him and his people? What was the root cause? Was it a spiritual attack? Was it fatigue?"

READING TIME

Read Chapter 3: "Diagnosing the Voodoo," in *The Panic Room*. Use the notes space to record any thoughts you want to remember or questions you want to talk about later.

How does it make you feel to know that there is One who perfectly understands every struggle and weakness you're experiencing?

_____

_____

_____

_____

_____

_____

What misconceptions have you encountered—both in leadership and in the church—when it comes to diagnosing problems, illnesses, and other struggles?

_____

_____

_____

_____

_____

Pastor Troy didn't know what to pray for—whether he was dealing with an evil spirit, a demonic attack, or a physical illness. What positive steps do you see him taking in this chapter, both with God and with others?

_____

_____

_____

_____

_____

_____

STUDY SCRIPTURE

Read Romans 8:22-27

"We know that the whole creation has been groaning as in the pains of childbirth right up to the present time. Not only so, but we ourselves, who have the firstfruits of the Spirit, groan inwardly as we wait eagerly for our adoption to sonship, the redemption of our bodies. For in this hope we were saved. But hope that is seen is no hope at all. Who hopes for what they already have? But if we hope for what we do not yet have, we wait for it patiently.

"In the same way, the Spirit helps us in our weakness. We do not know what we ought to pray for, but the Spirit himself intercedes for us through wordless groans. And he who searches our hearts knows the mind of the Spirit, because the Spirit intercedes for God's people in accordance with the will of God."

Think of a struggle you're currently facing, and write it below. Who is a person with experience in this area who can help to guide you and provide insight?

_____

_____

_____

_____

_____

_____

Why do you think the church especially, but society as a whole, has developed a strong stigma surrounding issues of mental health? How have you seen this manifest itself in the world around you?

_____

_____

_____

_____

_____

_____

_____

What do you see as the turning point for Pastor Troy in this chapter? What beliefs or assumptions did he need to overcome in order to get to that point?

_____

_____

_____

_____

_____

Why is it important that, both in his battle with panic attacks and his journey with his unborn daughter, Pastor Troy moved forward in faith even when he didn't have all the answers?

_____

_____

_____

_____

_____

_____

What are some answers or solutions you're currently searching for in your leadership journey?

_____

_____

_____

_____

_____

_____

What are a few practical, specific steps you can take to seek wisdom from God and others, and to step forward, even in the face of ambiguity?

_____

_____

_____

_____

_____

_____

_____

THE WALL

"I wish it had been a straight line from diagnosing th panic attacks to overcoming them with positive lifesty changes. It wasn't. The problems behind the attacks we a lot deeper than I knew."

READING TIME

Read Chapter 4: "The Wall," in *The Panic Room*. Use the notes space to record any thoughts you want to remember or questions you want to talk about later.

Why do you think it's difficult for leaders to admit that we don't have all the answers?

_____

_____

_____

_____

_____

_____

Have you ever cried out to God during a time of confusion and ambiguity? What did this time teach you? What were your main frustrations and questions?

_____

_____

_____

_____

_____

What value do you see in the journey between problem and solution? As a leader, how have you seen this space grow both you and your people?

_____

_____

_____

_____

_____

STUDY SCRIPTURE

Read 2 Corinthians 12:1-10

"I must go on boasting. Although there is nothing to be gained, I will go on to visions and revelations from the Lord. I know a man in Christ who fourteen years ago was caught up to the third heaven. Whether it was in the body or out of the body I do not know—God knows. And I know that this man—whether in the body or apart from the body I do not know, but God knows— was caught up to paradise and heard inexpressible things, things that no one is permitted to tell. I will boast about a man like that, but I will not boast about myself, except about my weaknesses. Even if I should choose to boast, I would not be a fool, because I would be speaking the truth. But I refrain, so no one will think more of me than is warranted by what I do or say, or because of these surpassingly great revelations. Therefore, in order to keep me from becoming conceited, I was given a thorn in my flesh, a messenger of Satan, to torment me. Three times I pleaded with the Lord to take it away from me. But he said to me, "My grace is sufficient for you, for my power is made perfect in weakness." Therefore I will boast all the more gladly about my weaknesses, so that Christ's power may rest on me. That is why, for Christ's sake, I delight in weaknesses, in insults, in hardships, in persecutions, in difficulties. For when I am weak, then I am strong."

Why is it so tempting to talk ourselves into an "I'm fine" mentality...until we hit the wall?

_____

_____

_____

_____

_____

How does Paul's conclusion about his weaknesses actually lead to freedom?

_____

_____

_____

_____

_____

Conversely, how does refusing to acknowledge our own weaknesses leave us enslaved?

_____

_____

_____

_____

_____

Leaders are excellent at vision-casting and inspiring our people...but we're not always so skilled at the execution part. How did Pastor Troy take action to combat his mental illness? What practical steps did he implement immediately?

_____

_____

_____

_____

_____

What practical steps can you take today, right now, to begin making positive changes in your life (it could be for your physical health, mental health, social life, leadership, etc.)?

_____

_____

_____

_____

_____

_____

Have you ever struggled with mental health before? If so, what have you learned from this experience? If not, what did you learn from this chapter about the interconnection between physical health and mental health?

_____

_____

_____

_____

_____

Why do you think, given the nature of the panic attacks he suffered, that Pastor Troy was so adamant about telling himself he was "fine"?

_____

_____

_____

_____

_____

_____

Are you leading in such a way that your people would feel comfortable coming to you with their struggles and weaknesses? Explain your answer.

_____

_____

_____

_____

_____

What's one way you can move towards cultivating a culture in which people are free to voice their need for help, their need for a break, or how they are honestly doing?

_____

_____

_____

_____

How do you think the church can improve in the way it creates this culture, and in the conversations it holds about mental health?

_____

_____

_____

_____

_____

ON THE OTHER
SIDE OF PANIC ATTACKS

"Robotically, I pressed through, not wanting to consider what I had become as a result of what had happened to Troy."

READING TIME

Read Chapter 5: "On the Other Side of Panic Attacks," in *The Panic Room*. Use the notes space to record any thoughts you want to remember or questions you want to talk about later.

Have you ever stood beside a close friend or family member who struggled with his or her mental health? What was this experience like for you, as a supporter/caretaker?

_____

_____

_____

_____

_____

_____

What struggles or challenges do family and/or someone's support network deal with in trying to support him or her during difficult times?

_____

_____

_____

_____

_____

_____

How did Pastor Penny allow herself to be inordinately burdened in the process of trying to care for her husband?

_____

_____

_____

_____

_____

_____

STUDY SCRIPTURE

Read 2 Corinthians 8:9-15

"For you know the grace of our Lord Jesus Christ, that though he was rich, yet for your sake he became poor, so that you by his poverty might become rich. And in this matter I give my judgment: this benefits you, who a year ago started not only to do this work but also to desire to do it. So now finish doing it as well, so that your readiness in desiring it may be matched by your completing it out of what you have. For if the readiness is there, it is acceptable according to what a person has, not according to what he does not have. For I do not mean that others should be eased and you burdened, but that as a matter of fairness your abundance at the present time should supply their need, so that their abundance may supply your need, that there may be fairness. As it is written, "Whoever gathered much had nothing left over, and whoever gathered little had no lack.""

Have you ever taken on too much in an effort to help another person—or even your organization? How does this actually do the opposite of helping?

_____

_____

_____

_____

_____

Have you ever denied a source of pain in your own leadership, relationships, or personal life? Was this an unconscious denial, or did you actively choose to ignore it?

_____

_____

_____

_____

_____

_____

Why do you think we tend to want the easiest, quickest way out of pain?

_____

_____

_____

_____

_____

What potential do pain and discomfort hold for us as leaders?

_____

_____

_____

_____

_____

SHARE YOUR STORY

"Until you experience enough pain, I've concluded, you deny that it's actually there."

Have you ever needed to support or help someone who was either parallel to you or above you in leadership? How did you navigate these waters respectfully and honestly?

_____

_____

_____

_____

_____

_____

How does insecurity cause us to misinterpret the intentions, words, and actions of others? How does it warp our own personal perspectives?

_____

_____

_____

_____

_____

What practical steps can you take to improve your relationships with your fellow leaders?

_____

_____

_____

_____

_____

_____

CHAPTER 6

FORCING
THE CONVERSATION

"Truth had won out. Troy wasn't broken. He was a normal human being doing extraordinary things. But for me getting back to normal took a little longer."

READING TIME

Read Chapter 6: "Forcing the Conversation," in *The Panic Room.* Use the notes space to record any thoughts you want to remember or questions you want to talk about later.

Have you ever needed to have a hard conversation with a coworker or fellow leader? What was it about?

_____

_____

_____

_____

_____

_____

_____

How did you go about navigating this conversation? Is there anything you would have done better, or that you learned from it?

_____

_____

_____

_____

_____

_____

Why was it so important that both Pastors Troy and Penny come to a place of humility and forgiveness for one another?

_____

_____

_____

_____

_____

_____

STUDY SCRIPTURE

Read Colossians 3:1-14

"Since, then, you have been raised with Christ, set your hearts on things above, where Christ is, seated at the right hand of God. Set your minds on things above, not on earthly things. For you died, and your life is now hidden with Christ in God. When Christ, who is your life, appears, then you also will appear with him in glory.

Put to death, therefore, whatever belongs to your earthly nature: sexual immorality, impurity, lust, evil desires and greed, which is idolatry. Because of these, the wrath of God is coming. You used to walk in these ways, in the life you once lived. But now you must also rid yourselves of all such things as these: anger, rage, malice, slander, and filthy language from your lips. Do not lie to each other, since you have taken off your old self with its practices and have put on the new self, which is being renewed in knowledge in the image of its Creator. Here there is no Gentile or Jew, circumcised or uncircumcised, barbarian, Scythian, slave or free, but Christ is all, and is in all.

Therefore, as God's chosen people, holy and dearly loved, clothe yourselves with compassion, kindness, humility, gentleness and patience. Bear with each other and forgive one another if any of you has a grievance against someone. Forgive as the Lord forgave you. And over all these virtues put on love, which binds them all together in perfect unity."

How do you think Pastor Penny's pain made it more difficult for her to "go back to normal," in some ways, than Pastor Troy?

_____

_____

_____

_____

_____

In your own words, why is confrontation and conflict so essential in leadership?

_____

_____

_____

_____

What risks do we run by avoiding or refusing to address conflict?

_____

_____

_____

_____

Do you tend to be someone who seeks out conflict, or who runs from it? Why do you think this is?

_____

_____

_____

_____

Why do you think it was especially difficult for Pastor Penny to be honest about her own struggles?

_____

_____

_____

_____

_____

_____

_____

What "panic room" might you be building for yourself, even if you aren't actually struggling with panic attacks or mental health? If you can't identify one currently, think about one you may have built for yourself in the past.

_____

_____

_____

_____

_____

WORKING TOGETHER AGAIN

"When we battle shame we don't give ourselves any room for God's grace. We instead run away from the help that we need. We end up hiding just like Adam and Eve."

READING TIME

Read Chapter 7: "Working Together Again," in *The Panic Room.* Use the notes space to record any thoughts you want to remember or questions you want to talk about later.

How do you think our tendency to hide our shame, instead of being open and honest with God and with others, is tied to Adam and Eve's decision to hide in the Garden of Eden?

_____

_____

_____

_____

_____

_____

_____

What do we miss out on when we hide from others and deceive ourselves?

_____

_____

_____

_____

_____

_____

What fears, struggles, and weaknesses has the Lord helped you overcome or persevere in the midst of? Take a few minutes to pray and thank Him for His goodness.

_____

_____

_____

_____

_____

_____

STUDY SCRIPTURE

Read Psalm 34:1-10

"I will extol the LORD at all times;
   his praise will always be on my lips.
I will glory in the LORD;
   let the afflicted hear and rejoice.
Glorify the LORD with me;
   let us exalt his name together.
I sought the LORD, and he answered me;
   he delivered me from all my fears.
Those who look to him are radiant;
   their faces are never covered with shame.
This poor man called, and the LORD heard him;
   he saved him out of all his troubles.
The angel of the LORD encamps around those who fear him,
   and he delivers them.
Taste and see that the LORD is good;
   blessed is the one who takes refuge in him.
Fear the LORD, you his holy people,
   for those who fear him lack nothing.
The lions may grow weak and hungry,
   but those who seek the LORD lack no good thing."

Who has helped you in the process of overcoming these difficulties and growing in the midst of your journey? Today, call or message them to express your gratitude.

_____

_____

_____

_____

_____

Have you ever relied on someone for things that only God could give you? What did that look like in your life?

_____

_____

_____

_____

_____

How did you come to realize the unhealthy expectations you were placing on that person/those people?

_____

_____

_____

_____

_____

_____

_____

What about currently—is there anyone you're depending on for too much, or placing unrealistic expectations on? How do you know?

_____

_____

_____

_____

_____

_____

Have you allowed someone else to place unrealistic expectations on you (or have you invited this by trying to be "all things" to others)?

_____

_____

_____

_____

_____

_____

What is the hardest part of recognizing, admitting, and surrendering shame for you personally? Where do you tend to get caught up in shame?

_____

_____

_____

_____

_____

Find 1-2 key Scripture verses or passages that speak to God's grace, forgiveness, and identity over your life. Write them down and put them where you can will them every day.

_____

_____

_____

_____

_____

What's one thing you need to stop feeling ashamed of right now? Write a prayer surrendering this thing to God, thanking Him for His goodness, and accepting His forgiveness, mercy, and grace toward you.

_____

_____

_____

_____

_____

CHAPTER 8

OUT OF THE PANIC ROOM

"The enemy's plan ever since [Adam and Eve] has been to push individuals into isolation, into panic rooms where we are weak and vulnerable."

READING TIME

Read Chapter 8: "Out of the Panic Room," in *The Panic Room*. Use the notes space to record any thoughts you want to remember or questions you want to talk about later.

Have you ever endured a season of isolation? What are the main factors that you believe led to that time of loneliness?

_____

_____

_____

_____

_____

_____

_____

As a leader, what are some ways you are better with a support network in place? How do others help you grow, improve, and learn?

_____

_____

_____

_____

_____

_____

What weaknesses did the paralyzed man have to be open about with his friends, the crowd, and Jesus in order to receive healing?

_____

_____

_____

_____

_____

_____

STUDY SCRIPTURE

Read Mark 2:1-12

"A few days later, when Jesus again entered Capernaum, the people heard that he had come home. They gathered in such large numbers that there was no room left, not even outside the door, and he preached the word to them. Some men came, bringing to him a paralyzed man, carried by four of them. Since they could not get him to Jesus because of the crowd, they made an opening in the roof above Jesus by digging through it and then lowered the mat the man was lying on. When Jesus saw their faith, he said to the paralyzed man, 'Son, your sins are forgiven.'

Now some teachers of the law were sitting there, thinking to themselves, 'Why does this fellow talk like that? He's blaspheming! Who can forgive sins but God alone?'

Immediately Jesus knew in his spirit that this was what they were thinking in their hearts, and he said to them, 'Why are you thinking these things? Which is easier: to say to this paralyzed man, "Your sins are forgiven," or to say, "Get up, take your mat and walk"? But I want you to know that the Son of Man has authority on earth to forgive sins.' So he said to the man, 'I tell you, get up, take your mat and go home.' He got up, took his mat and walked out in full view of them all. This amazed everyone and they praised God, saying, 'We have never seen anything like this!'"

What weaknesses, struggles, and shortcomings have you been hiding from those around you that you need to be more open about?

_____

_____

_____

_____

Think about your family, close friends, and your team. How have you learned more about who God is because of them?

_____

_____

_____

_____

How have these individuals taught you more about yourself?

_____

_____

_____

_____

What's one way you can help someone else learn more about themselves— either you personally or by providing them with resources, connections, training, etc.?

_____

_____

_____

_____

_____

SHARE YOUR STORY

"Community helps us discover who God is and who we are. The clearer we see him, the clearer we see ourselves."

Why do you think the panic room causes us to believe that we're okay (or even better off) without others?

_____

_____

_____

_____

_____

_____

_____

Do you struggle to trust others in any specific area of your life? If so, what is it?

_____

_____

_____

_____

_____

_____

What do you stand to gain by being vulnerable in this area? What might you have to sacrifice (how might vulnerability be uncomfortable for you)?

_____

_____

_____

_____

_____

_____

In your own words, explore how your purpose is intertwined with the people around you. What might you fail to realize or achieve without others supporting you? What might others fail to achieve without your support?

_____

_____

_____

_____

_____

CHAPTER 9

REST IS A WEAPON

"My inability to rest sprang from a struggle with my own identity...I was focused on justifying my existence, proving my success."

READING TIME

Read Chapter 9: "Rest Is a Weapon," in *The Panic Room*. Use the notes space to record any thoughts you want to remember or questions you want to talk about later.

Why do you believe so many leaders find it difficult to take a day off, let alone a vacation or sabbatical?

_____

_____

_____

_____

_____

_____

Are there any societal, cultural, or other factors that influence this mindset for leaders like you?

_____

_____

_____

_____

_____

_____

What is the significance of the fact that God modeled the Sabbath for us when He Himself took a day to rest at the end of creation?

_____

_____

_____

_____

_____

_____

STUDY SCRIPTURE

Read Exodus 20:8-11

"Remember the Sabbath day by keeping it holy. Six days you shall labor and do all your work, but the seventh day is a sabbath to the LORD your God. On it you shall not do any work, neither you, nor your son or daughter, nor your male or female servant, nor your animals, nor any foreigner residing in your towns. For in six days the LORD made the heavens and the earth, the sea, and all that is in them, but he rested on the seventh day. Therefore the LORD blessed the Sabbath day and made it holy."

What are some key opportunities that rest gives us that we can't enjoy when we're working?

_____

_____

_____

_____

_____

In your own words, why is refusing to rest actually counterproductive?

_____

_____

_____

_____

_____

What do you think it says to others when you refuse to take a break? What do you think it says about your view of God?

_____

_____

_____

_____

_____

How do you think rest can be a weapon leaders use to grow, stay healthy, and be even more successful?

_____

_____

_____

_____

_____

What things does rest free us from? What has it freed you from?

_____

_____

_____

_____

_____

SHARE YOUR STORY

"One of the hardest lessons to learn was that for every yes there has to be a no somewhere."

Do you find it easy or difficult to take days or weeks off of work? Why do you think that is?

_____

_____

_____

_____

_____

_____

_____

What is your plan/routine for taking time off? How frequently do you have days off (weekly, biweekly, etc.)? What about extended breaks such as week-long vacations or sabbaticals?

_____

_____

_____

_____

_____

_____

What are 2-3 practical ways you can improve the rest/vacation culture in your workplace? How can you influence those you lead to enjoy, take advantage of, and look forward to their times of rest?

_____

_____

_____

_____

_____

_____

CHAPTER 10

I'M NOT ALONE

"The goal is to find God in the middle of our mess. The Holy Spirit actually wants to be invited into the negative stuff you've got going on."

READING TIME

Read Chapter 10: "I'm Not Alone," in *The Panic Room.* Use the notes space to record any thoughts you want to remember or questions you want to talk about later.

Has God ever asked you to share about a season of vulnerability with others? If so, how did that experience grow or change you?

_____

_____

_____

_____

_____

_____

_____

What Biblical figures can you think of who endured times of anxiety, depression, discouragement, or otherwise "messy" states of being?

_____

_____

_____

_____

_____

_____

Why do you think God so often chose to use weak, messy people to show Himself to the world?

_____

_____

_____

_____

_____

_____

_____

STUDY SCRIPTURE

Read Mark 2:13-17

"Once again Jesus went out beside the lake. A large crowd came to him, and he began to teach them. As he walked along, he saw Levi son of Alphaeus sitting at the tax collector's booth. 'Follow me,' Jesus told him, and Levi got up and followed him.

While Jesus was having dinner at Levi's house, many tax collectors and sinners were eating with him and his disciples, for there were many who followed him. When the teachers of the law who were Pharisees saw him eating with the sinners and tax collectors, they asked his disciples: 'Why does he eat with tax collectors and sinners?'

On hearing this, Jesus said to them, 'It is not the healthy who need a doctor, but the sick. I have not come to call the righteous, but sinners.'"

What weaknesses of yours might God want to use to show Himself to those around you in a new way?

_____

_____

_____

_____

_____

How does it change your perception of God to know that He wants to be invited into the messy parts of your life? How does this make you feel?

_____

_____

_____

_____

_____

Are there any areas of your life in which you haven't invited the Holy Spirit to intervene? Why do you think you've held these areas back from Him?

_____

_____

_____

_____

_____

How do you need God to intervene in these areas and work in ways that you can't?

_____

_____

_____

_____

_____

_____

What are some qualities and aspects of God's character that you want to become well-acquainted with?

_____

_____

_____

_____

_____

_____

_____

Write a prayer asking the Holy Spirit to invade every area of your life, surrendering to Him, and thanking Him for wanting to be intimately acquainted with you.

_____

_____

_____

_____

_____

_____

_____

CPSIA information can be obtained
at www.ICGtesting.com
Printed in the USA
BVHW030443260821
614578BV00003B/6